I0621790

ENDSCAPE

_hydrus

Published by: Hydrus

Photography, Cover Art & Illustrated Art by: Hydrus

Cover Design by: Cleo Moran - Devoted Pages Designs

Formatting by: Cleo Moran - Devoted Pages Designs

https://www.devotedpages.com

Proofreading by: Amina Jojo Dahmouche

Manufactured in the United States of America

The Library of Congress Cataloging-in-Publication Data is available upon request.

E-Book Isbn: 979-8-9913977-0-4

Paperback Isbn: 979-8-9913977-1-1

Dedicated to those of us who can't get away

—H

ENDscape

In ENDscape, I found myself writing about the experience of being lost, yet always yearning to be found. It reflects the desire to escape the darkness, even when a part of us is drawn to linger in it. Every corner of our minds holds a mirror to life's most profound struggles.

These poems delve into the weight of feeling trapped, the silent battles fought within the shadows of the soul, and the relentless yearning for an escape that always seems just beyond reach. Whether we confront these struggles head-on, evade them, or carry them silently within us, they are burdens we all bear.

ENDscape seeks to capture the raw bursts of emotion that arise in these moments-haunting thoughts and feelings that emerge from deep within our own minds. It explores the inner turmoil that often intertwines with self-doubt, weaving a tapestry of the human experience.

You hid in lies
Only to be unseen by love_

_hydrus

Break to be broken
Love was not wept
Sorrow is unspoken
Sadness never kept

Fragment
_hydrus

I am judged by my wrongs
When they felt so right

_hydrus

Your silence broke
The heart you filled
You now can rest
In what you killed

Piece
_hydrus

Pain is remembering
To never forget
A constant reminder
Of countless regrets

Time not cherished
Words unspokenly said
Moments now vanished
A love declared dead

Tragedy
_hydrus

Our reality was born the day
we were not one

_hydrus

As you sleep
I dream of you
Endless thoughts
And all are true

Wishing you rest
Just next to me
Upon my chest
I pray you be

Ether
_hydrus

Waiting for the storm to pass
My mind plays all its tricks
Drowning in what will not last
Questioning why I'm sick

Homeland
_hydrus

I find myself hiding in silence
After losing you became my home
      _hydrus

I focused on what was wrong
Without being able to see
_hydrus

Never feeling good enough
Life can be so cruel
The mirror haunts my every look
Spilling as a fool

Cracked
_hydrus

You are everything I wanted
And all that I don't deserve

_hydrus

Broken hearts
From a silenced song
A quiet note
When all went wrong

The music stopped
No more romance
We lost a soul
To a pointless dance

Constellation
_hydrus

Every leaf
As it drops
Is another tear
That never stops

hydrus

I found in you
A perfect soul
The thunderous fire
Out of control

Burned alive
My heart you stole
Forever yours
You made me whole

Puzzle
_hydrus

Love lives
In another place
A stranger's hands
Leaving their trace

Sitting alone
As the heart lies
Words are spoken
Inside I die

Spew
_hydrus

I drink my ghosts
To forget I am dead

_hydrus

Left for forgotten
In the bed that you made
The roses now rotten
As I dwell in my cave

Sadness now dripping
In the walls carved of bone
Pain replaces all feeling
Memories fade into stone

Glyph
_hydrus

There is nothing
Without our something
_hydrus

In my heart
There resides a bliss
A person I cherish
Whom is dearly miss

I awake alone
She's no longer there
Her morning kisses
Fueled in despair

She was my cauldron
An endless night
Her ravened presence
Never far from sight

The search continues
Until the day
She returns from flight
With me to stay

Ruin
_hydrus

Don't look back
I will always be here for you

_hydrus

Pointed fingers
A speared decay
Judged in silence
Venom sprayed

Lost emotion
Demons raid
Reckless notions
Vision fades

Blurred
_hydrus

In his arms
Slowly it beats
A stranger's love
Buried so deep

Far away
Trapped in a cell
Prisoned hope
You won't expel

Hypocrite
_hydrus

You are the death I want to keep reliving
_hydrus

I exist to miss you
Dread what I lost
Unable to handle
Not knowing the cost

Only your memory
Burns in my flame
Together was not forever
I hunger your name

Illusion
_hydrus

Drain me of my soul
So we can lose self control

_hydrus

Sometimes the mind just wins
When the heart fails

_hydrus

You are the endless
Sunset
That rises
On my darkest days

Flare
_hydrus

My death lives in your remains

_hydrus

I cannot navigate
See beyond the storms
Heavy pounding rains
Wash upon my horns

Defiantly awaiting
My ending will appear
While quietly deceiving
Alone to face my fears

Shallows
_hydrus

I was the game
You prepped to use
Groomed my love
Just to amuse

My heart was open
Gave you my faith
Your dark intentions
Sealed our fate

Signed
_hydrus

I felt your soul
As it touched mine
You felt so close
It was divine

But the light came in
Blinded my sight
I awoke again
To my constant night

Wasn't
_hydrus

Thinking of you
Even when I mustn't.

_hydrus

Evil wins
When you lose control
Playing games
With your soul

Keep it far
Without any trust
Once inside
It thrives on lust

Groomed
_hydrus

I need you here
Only with me
Remove the leash
Throw away the keys

My heart is begging
For you to come
Take my hand
Let's just be one

If you don't come
I will understand
The stars are broken
So is your man

Until our souls
Meet up again
Hoping this time
We wouldn't end

Boarded
_hydrus

I will catch you
Bind the hands
Undress your body
Tortured commands

Spread your demons
Inject my lies
Crown this madness
Between your thighs

Lashes
_hydrus

Tell me all your secrets
Then let's create some lies
Venom between our lips
Watching others die

Slowly we will creep
Sever every wound
Seep into all their dreams
Leave them all confused

Swarm
_hydrus

Only she could hear me moan
Fuck me
Under my breath

_hydrus

Don't get passed around
When you should be one's only choice

_hydrus

Far you went
Away from me
Stole my heart
Erased the key

Unlocked a love
I found in you
An endless heaven
You are my truth

Lie
_hydrus

I will carry you
Until my footsteps bleed
_hydrus

Not a day goes by
That I don't think of you
You filled my soul
The oceans were blue

Surrendering to passion
Reality would undo
I lost my way
Then I lost you

Waveless
_hydrus

Night arrives
I am on my way
Beneath the moon
And the sun's decay

Teeth are sharpened
Prepped to bite
In my hands
You won't take flight

Minutes
_hydrus

Sometimes madness
Finds a home
When we feel
We are all alone

It digs its claws
Rips the skin
Reminds the earth
Of all our sin

Unholy
_hydrus

ENDscape

In this life
I met my soul
It drove the dagger
That took control

She claimed my heart
But she wasn't mine
I guess the joke
Was there all the time

Smoke & Mirrors
hydrus

ENDscape

In every smile
I no longer make
Lives the sadness
Of my mistakes

_hydrus

Holding on to us
Then practicing goodbyes
Lonely hearts clutch
Desperately they cry

Every chapter ends
Nothing left to speak
Voices never mend
Love has made us weak

Sold
_hydrus

No one shares
What gives you life

_hydrus

I found a flower
Covered in dust
Her petals raw
Drained of trust

The clouds would come
Drop all their rain
The little flower
Would wilt in pain

More clouds arrived
As the showers grew
The sun would watch
Thought it was cute

What fun these clouds
Would have in shame
I wished them harm
It was their game

Savages
_hydrus

When I lost her
To someone else
I never found
My real true self

_hydrus

I am reminded of death
Every time
You bring me back to life

Hell
_hydrus

Don't you know
You are missed
The hours pass
We still can't kiss

Time depraves
Taunts my heart
I never want
You to part

Ways
_hydrus

Staring at you
Your eyes they tease
They call for me
I want to please

Your begging lips
Curves and shape
Whisper secrets
For me to take

Upon your hips
I lay my tongue
Slowly tracing
The trail I've won

Under your dress
You feel me rise
Big hands grab all
Taking their prize

Making your mess
Smothered in place
Grinding such bliss
Upon my face

Feel me enter
More ways than one
I want you dripping
Until the morning sun

Cake
_hydrus

Let's get lost in your garden
Let's compose another song
Sing to every petal
Dance where I belong

Synced
_hydrus

Every nightmare began with me losing you
because of me

_hydrus

Knowing you are not mine
In his arms you wake
Living life without you
Paying for my mistakes

Debt
_hydrus

If only you knew
What you meant to me
I never had a clue
Of how we needed to be

Stubborn in my ways
I'm to blame for it all
Living out my days
Secluded from the fall

Cut
_hydrus

Don't tell me that I matter
When your heart beats for someone else

_hydrus

Listen
That's me thinking about you
Question
Are you thinking about me

Mood
_hydrus

Another day
Slow it begins
Need to drown
Away my sins

Quitting
_hydrus

I see you
In every stare
Feel you far
But I don't care

Need to breathe you
Life's not fair
Soon I'll feed you
Inside your lair

Bones
_hydrus

The knots you made
Reminded me of the ropes you spun
_hydrus

Life gives so much
Then strips away
Leaves you barren
No words to say

In that darkness
Lives a light
It keeps you fighting
For what is right

Floating
_hydrus

I am wed to the earth
For its bed awaits my descent

_hydrus

Every tree
That I could climb
Would never be
Enough in time

If I reach
The top one day
Our leaves would fall
And just decay

Saw
_hydrus

Beneath the stars
The moon and mars
The rivers fall
And open scars

They bleed away
Wash the decay
The open wounds
Will heal real soon

Spawn
_hydrus

75'

My heart surrendered
Then I failed
Drowning our future
Left us impaled

Treason
_hydrus

You are not someone's pastime
To be uselessly passed off as a hobby

_hydrus

Savage mane
Dresses fists
Tightly pulled
Clenching grips

Arching howls
Embedded claws
A ravaged den
Skin is mauled

Carnivore
_hydrus

I can't imagine
A life without you
Etched inside
You are my truth

You melt away
My scars and fears
Give me life
When all was tears

Flood
_hydrus

Pretty eyes speak
Of haunted dreams
Now he's become
The shiny thing

What everyone wants
To rip and smear
Used as the trash
That he once feared

Became
_hydrus

I want to relive
The moment we knew
Fate was reality

_hydrus

Life broke my heart
When I realized
It was too far away
For me to love

Swifted
_hydrus

Let's pick up the pieces
That we have yet made broken

_hydrus

I knew pain would become my only friend
The moment you walked away from us

_hydrus

We danced in the rain
Made the puddles blush
Swam in each other's arms
More than just a crush

Soon you went away
The sun would burn the sky
Never mine to love
Our time was just a lie

Aimless
_hydrus

Sleep evades
Slumber fails
The mind plays tricks
Telling me tales

Winter dreams
Restless nights
A foggy mist
Clouds my sight

Next to me
His gallows rest
A mocking heart
My beating pest

If the day
Shall not appear
Joy will return
Without a tear

Cased
_hydrus

Not a moment passes
That I don't sink
Into my thoughts
Where sadness drinks

You are with another
And not with me
I cannot live
I will not be

Honest
_hydrus

ENDscape

Vultures love to see you fall
Envy you when you fly
They perch around your empty corpse
To laugh at why you died

Scavengers
_hydrus

90

The heart
Left me nowhere
And my somewhere
Was being alone

Absent
_hydrus

Follow me
Into my lair
Restless ghosts
Bring you here

Close your eyes
See what awaits
Open wide
And watch me taste

Wail
_hydrus

Why
Did you leave
I was broken
And deceived

Unwilling
And distressed
Unable to live
Or just confess

My days were empty
You didn't stay
But we drifted
Drifted so far away

Now I am lost
Paying the cost
Forever tortured
When lines were crossed

Ruse
_hydrus

You hide in darkness
Its muse your tact
Just a sad relic
For your wretched acts

All on display
Holes full of flags
Your clowns now play
Laugh as you gag

Dumpster
_hydrus

I never knew
I would hurt like this
Face in hands
In my abyss

The light has faded
All notes don't sing
Living in darkness
Torn my wings

Collapsed
_hydrus

Tightening my hands
Tracing your steps
Beyond these hills
I hear your breath

Closer I get
Tingling your spine
Do not slow down
Or I'll take what's mine

Heartbeat
_hydrus

In my eyes
Your soul's complete
It won my heart
I claimed defeat

Upon your sword
I'm a conquered land
Serving your crown
And your demands

Fallen serpent
Dressed as a ram
Hidden misfortunes
Buried in sand

Stars will align
Forget what you thirst
Spit your disgrace
Born to be cursed

Bloodline
_hydrus

Swallow my heart
Devour my life
Kiss your thief
I do whatever you like

Sanctuary
_hydrus

I made the fear of losing you
Reality when I did

_hydrus

Eerie voices
Fill the room
Under sheets
Lies a groom

Unaware
Of his bedded mate
She lays silent
Having met her fate

Don't Stare
_hydrus

Even when I die
I will be alive

In the stars
And the empty skies

I will live
My soul will thrive

Even when I die
I will survive

Firm
_hydrus

A garden's life
Gratitude's seed
Bloom that blossoms
In every good deed

Rivers flow
Let's thank the cascade
Gratefulness reigns
Never let it just fade

Gem
_hydrus

ENDScape

I miss you as much as I breathe

and think of you when I don't _hydrus

Little bird
With broken wings
In the sky you tumble
No longer sings

Amongst the clouds
You fly to hide
The nest is empty
And so dark inside

Flutter
_hydrus

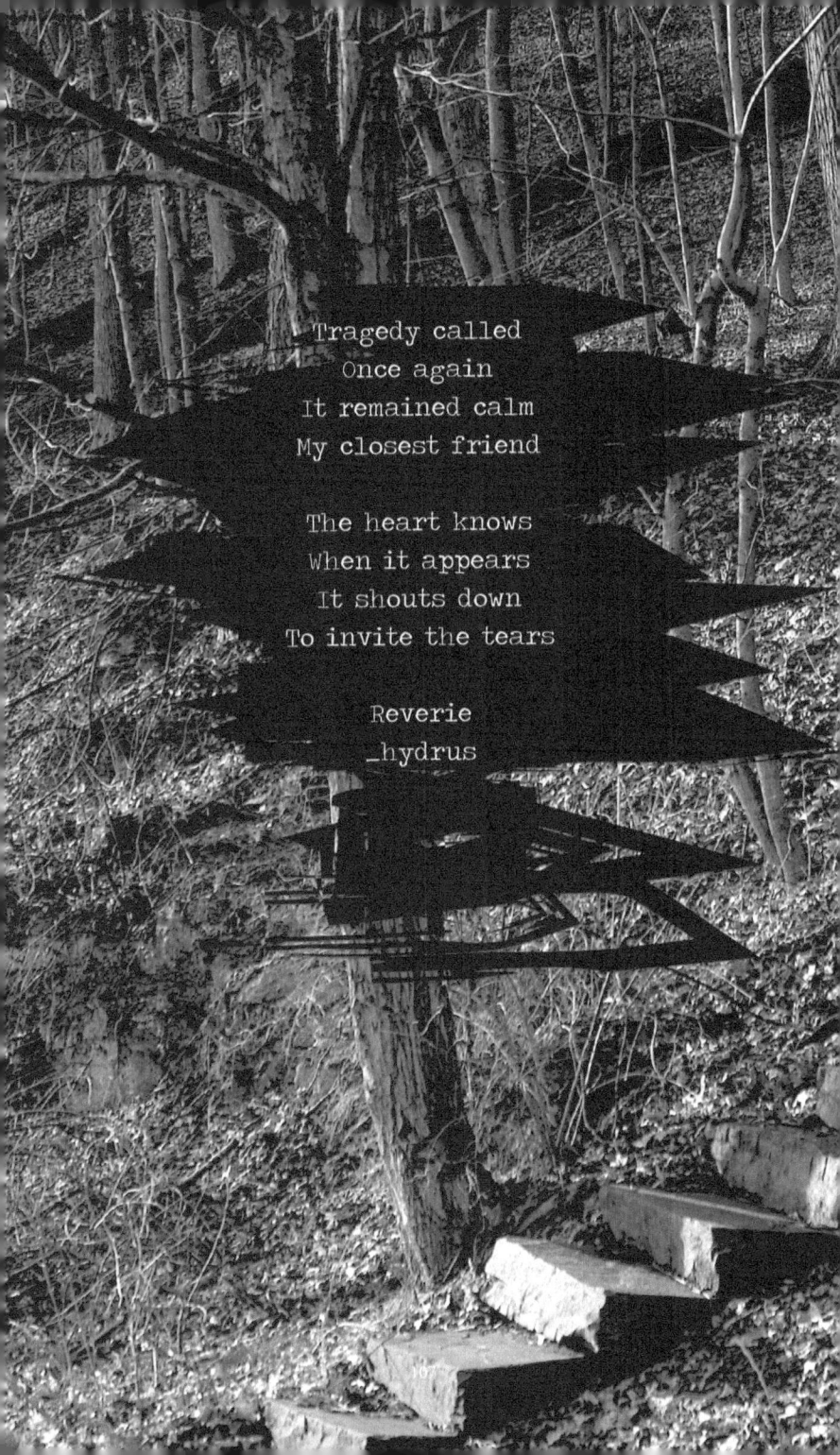

Tragedy called
Once again
It remained calm
My closest friend

The heart knows
When it appears
It shouts down
To invite the tears

Reverie
_hydrus

Every morning
That I awake
I think of you
And the smiles you make

You are my world
Nothing I've known
A love so pure
Slowly we've grown

Away from me
Yet in my heart
You claimed each space
And every part

A constant heaven
Every day reborn
Good luck my baby
I'm forever yours

My Everything
_hydrus

Through the trees
I hear the breeze
The world I love
My heart it feeds

Taking all in
Recharging to grow
Every seed it plants
Is the future we know

Blossom
_hydrus

Days go by
Without a trace
The heart is cold
An empty space

Memories of us
And all we shared
Are shadows now
Like no one cared

Rewritten
_hydrus

Winter is here
It knew my name
It casted doubts
Played its games

Haunted me
With owls and rain
Winter's here
To revive my pain

Horned
_hydrus

Again, a crow
Screams my name
Plucking the eyes
Scratching one's brain

Everything is mental
Going insane
Lost in their laughter
Cursed by this game

Poker
_hydrus

Traga mi corazón
Cómeme la vida
Besa a tu ladrón
Yo hago lo que pidas

Mio
_hydrus

113

Find your way
Back to me
On my knees
I beg and plead

Take my leash
Tie the hands
Ride your beast
Moan commands

Offering
_hydrus

Obsessed the vision
Of an empty skull
Silence drowns
Your every call

Within the walls
Of my shattered glass
Empty rooms
Haunt my past

Vacancy
_hydrus

Knowing that
He touches your skin
Awakes the demon
The wolf within

The anger that boils
Froths as you play
Sharpens the blade
Every moment you stay

Froth
_hydrus

Love remembers
What the heart forgets
Lives in forever
Tasting all regrets
Time's been lost
Feelings are spent
Missing what was
And what wasn't meant

Evoked
_hydrus

Lay me down
Give me my drug
Erase my thoughts
Of what once was

Addict
_hydrus

I left the sun
Burned from the star
The sky was open
So were my scars

Floating in space
What can one do
To reach the moon
And be with you

Mars
_hydrus

I don't have thoughts
Other than you
You consume my world
And make life new

Our earth is peace
You understand
I live for you
I am your man

Fated
_hydrus

She stares at his beard
He looks towards her way
Stroking his hair
Their eyes start to play

His lips start to tease
Whispering her name
She glides towards his lap
To continue their game

Dish
_hydrus

On the wall
There it hangs
Iron and steel
At my demand

In my hands
Taunts a voice
Giving me
No other choice

Enough
_hydrus

I ache for words
Any sound you make
An endless tunnel
Of our grand escape

Your moans and sighs
The laughs and quirks
Make my heart complete
It removes the hurt

Aid
_hydrus

You broke my heart
A million ways
Torn every petal
Dug up my grave

I gave you me
And became the fool
Six feet under
Based on your rule

Shovel
_hydrus

I never found myself
Once you were gone
It was my fault
And I was wrong

Volition
_hydrus

Glance at me
Look in my eyes
Life is complete
For you I die

I live in heaven
With each breath I take
You by my side
Every day I wake

Complete
_hydrus

Heaven opened
Shared you with me
My dark angel
Answered my pleas

She was magic
But I hid the sun
Fear took over
Our song was done

Horns
_hydrus

I watch and wait
To hear your voice
Time escapes
You made your choice

You chose another
As I burn in place
My heart retreated
And sealed my fate

Solitude
_hydrus

ENDscape

You make it easy to love

_hydrus

Away from me
Far from home
You gave me life
Now left alone

We cannot be
Must change our course
Without your love
Without remorse

Protect
_hydrus

If only I could reach
The parts of you that are broken
I would mend them with the tenderness
Of your soul

_hydrus

Why is nighttime such a friend
Yet I feel so alone by its presence

_hydrus

In a distant place
You lay awake
As I do the same
Thinking of mistakes

If only time
Could erase the past
I would find a way
To win you back

Repented
_hydrus

My heart never healed after you left
It only opened itself to being alone

_hydrus

The one I love
And always miss
Who leaves me breathless
With every kiss

Come back home
My heart still bleeds
Don't be alone
You are all I need

Distantly Blue
_hydrus

What an angel
Wings and allure
She is heavens' gift
A heart so pure

But this creature
Drowns in her lies
It lets the beasts
Come all inside

Vessel
_hydrus

Your fingers taste
Of every sin
We moaned

Cored
_hydrus
142

I found the sun
It brought the rain
My clouds grew dark
Fearing the pain

But in those storms
I felt her touch
It gave me hope
I miss her so much

Pushed
_hydrus

ENDscape

Chance not fate
Brought you to me
It saw through all
Of what should be

You are perfection
My destiny
Chance not fate
Brought you to me

Silhouette
_hydrus

ENDscape

After our storm
I could not heal
Feeling lost
Craving the steel

Caverns caved
Tore at my veins
The open wounds
Red ink stained

Walked
_hydrus

Let's escape
Redo our ink
Away from chaos
What people think

Start a new chapter
The world our stage
Erase all caution
Defile each page

Conditioned
_hydrus

How did you become
One with the dirt
Gnawing my emotions
To see me hurt

You set me up
And played me well
Hope you crawl
Back into hell

Beast
_hydrus

Beastly passion
Ignites the skin
Carnal ways
His hungry sin

Upon the flesh
Tongues trace the trail
Licking sips
To wag his tail

Trained
_hydrus

I was never good enough
Only good for you

_hydrus

I remained too much inside my head and
ended up losing my mind

Edgar Allan Poe

Even the loneliest fields bear fruit

_hydrus

THANK YOU

I want to express my deepest love and appreciation to all of you who have been following and supporting my poetry and ink. Your presence makes my writing journey incredibly meaningful, turning it into something beyond what I ever envisioned. I cannot thank you enough for the love, kindness, encouragement, and inspiration you've brought into my life!

A special thank you goes out to my amazing team of Cleo & Jojo. Your relentless dedication, support, and love mean everything to me. I know I'm not always the best at communicating or being accessible, but you both consistently manage to draw me out of my cave. I'm also immensely grateful for your patience, especially when my timelines surprise you. You are the engine behind Hydrus, and I feel exceptionally fortunate to have you by my side.

And another special thank You to my Ravens and to the Hydrus Team (ARC Readers), for your continuous love and support. Your creativity, passion, and kindness are integral to everything I do. I am constantly amazed by your contributions, beautiful and artistic creations and I can never adequately express how much gratitude I have for all that you do.

ENDSCAPE

Playlist

Poetry	Wrabel
Skinny Love	Birdy
Somewhere Only We Know	Rhianne
Signs of the Times	Harry Styles
It'll Be Okay	Shawn Mendes
I miss you, I'm sorry	Gracie Abrams
Forever	Noah Kahan
Burning Out	Hayd
Ghost Town	Benson Boone
THE LONELIEST	Måneskin
Lost My Mind	FINNEAS
Die Alone	FINNEAS
Soulmate	Chanin
Moon	Austin Giorgio
Would Anyone Care	Citizen Soldier
better off without me	Matt Hansen
Atlantis	Seafret
Next To You	John Vincent III
All The Same	SICK PUPPIES
Lies Lies Lies	Morgan Wallen
Rain	Sleep Token
Don't Forget Me	Imagine Dragons
HEAD OVER HEELS	Gun Boi Kaz
The Reason I Stay	Abby Anderson

Listen here:
bit.ly/3X5r5pt

Also by: _hydrus

ENDVISIBLE

A collection of poems about the endless feeling of being invisible while going through the emotions and sometimes cruelties of life. Illustrated by the author's own photography, this book guides us through grief, loss and love in a dark and inspiring way typical to how Hydrus's writing helps us cope with reality.

AWAK**END**

Tarots cards, much like poems, have the ability to paint a vivid picture of what once was or what could be. They delve into the subtleties that we all carry within ourselves and the secrets that make us who we are.

AwakEND is an immersion into the world of tarot and its mysteries. Read it one way, then another, and let the words guide you into the meaning of each card.
Allow chance and curiosity to accompany you on this incredible journey and let your heart awaken to hope even after having thought everything was lost...

And who knows what secrets you might find out about yourself...

DARK**END**

Is a small look into the world I call my reality.
Through poems, photography and art, I try to capture the ups and downs of this voyage we call life, and sometimes I refer to it as just existing.
Embedded in my words are stories of emotions and feelings that range from the darkest of moments to times of having some type of hope for resolve.

Life is raw and ever-evolving, and we always seem to put ourselves last overall. Time proves to be quite relentless. I hope that we all find common ground through our everyday struggles and in the end, understand that love, although painful at times, can provide so many answers.

So the question then becomes "how can we better love ourselves?"

HEART**END**

Is about how we experience love and some of the journeys we embark on when love strikes our heart. It's about the numerous complex phases and ever changing stages of the purest human emotions.
It might be a first kiss, a new romance, a guilty pleasure or a sense of loss but love always helps us reach the heavens or crash down upon its shores.
Love gives even when it takes, it heals and embeds its mark and sculpts us into who we are.

"We all open our hearts and in the end this is the love we bleed."
_hydrus

ENDTHOLOGY

Is a collection of poems drawn up from experiences, thoughts, and emotions. Not everything in the world is dark, but many times we live without any light. We lose ourselves in what we consider our reality. Our souls forget what is important. At the same time, we rejoice when we regain our passion and our inner light.

We might live many lives, but which one will you always remember?

What memories will we ink?

What will have true meaning?

How will we live our END?

_hydrus

A collection of poems that deal with the human struggle of being in love. The emotional roller coaster and the ups and downs that our souls take on this journey. This path is one of endless bliss but some-times agony.

Love is always a conflict of raw emotion and trust. It is a journey we seek to take and at times we regret we do. It is a struggle between good vs. evil but mostly in ourselves.

ENDROAD

An original collection of poetry, comprised of new works, writings, and photography. It documents the many facets of ones inner journey. It deals with our ever-changing emotions, and how the mind and heart react differently when confronted by lifes cruel ironies.

We all live inside and outside ourselves. The quiet whispers we hear and the ones we ignore. The inner voice that makes us passionate, gives us hope, or creates the monster that sharpens their teeth.

ENDroad details the winding aspects of that search for answers. It shows that we all sometimes feel the same. That we are not alone. The paths we take or the ones that take us to mold our humanity into who we are. Each one presents us with the ability for us to rediscover ourselves again.

At times we might feel lost but the truth to finding our way will always rest in our hearts.

My end does not mean I am finished
It only reveals that I am starting again.
_hydrus

WEAK**END**

What happens when life and love clash?
When desire is blinding and passion betrays?
Who do you become and where does it all END?

Welcome to WeakEND, the first book in the FallEND series.

Where we discover a man's journey to answer these questions.

"**Love gave so it could take**" and only his inner demons will keep
him from his angels. _hydrus

BROK**END**

Will he ever be able to recover?
Will he be able to find redemption or have a chance at finding
true love again?
Or will life just continue to ruin his hopes of finding true
happiness.

Sometimes the universe speaks to us in waves, only to watch us
drown in its infinite choir of noise. _hydrus

ENDFINITY

Everyone deserves love, understanding, to be heard, and, above all, hope.

As I began to write this book, penning thoughts and ideas about this very notion, I found myself in a place where the world sometimes appears overwhelmingly dark. I believe our minds and hearts resonate with that darkness too. Surrounded by negativity, often stemming from those around us, we may begin to doubt ourselves and our convictions.

I hope that by reading this book, you can find some direction, motivation, or perhaps even inspiration. A glimmer of light during dark and challenging times. I hope you will recognize that we all possess our own beauty. That each and every one of us has the power to shape our own destinies, rewrite our own stories, and uncover the true beauty that resides within us all. There is so much to explore, see, and experience out there. Our own horizons are limitless and vast.

We all deserve to venture and pursue our own happiness, and it begins with the infinite ways we need to believe in and love ourselves.

About The Author

Hydrus, is an enigmatic poet shrouded in mystery, who is also a photographer and artist. Within the veiled depths of anonymity, Hydrus pens verses that intricately capture the dance between darkness and the fleeting glimmers of light beyond the shadows. Having authored 10 books, his literary creations have traversed borders, resonating in over 30 countries. His words encompass the vast spectrum of human experience, exploring themes of love, loss, passion, triumph, inspiration, and darkness. Notably, he coined the phrase 'Write your Soul®,' encapsulating the belief that we all can right ourselves through the power of the written word.

Connect with _hydrus:

Website: www.hydruspoetry.com
Instagram: @hydruspoetry
Facebook: www.facebook.com/hydruspoetry
TikTok: @hydrus_ravens
Redbubble Merchandise:
www.redbubble.com/people/hydruspoetry/explore
YouTube:
https://www.youtube.com/@HydrusPoetry

I was lost just to be found
_hydrus